scarves
- a Knitter's dozen

a production of  *BOOKS*

i

Scarves; A Knitter's dozen PUBLISHED BY XRX BOOKS

Credits

PUBLISHER
Alexis Yiorgos Xenakis

COEDITORS
Rick Mondragon
Elaine Rowley

EDITORIAL ASSISTANT
Sue Nelson

INSTRUCTION EDITOR
Joni Coniglio

INSTRUCTION ASSISTANTS
Cole Kelley
Ashley Mercer

GRAPHIC DESIGNER
Bob Natz

PHOTOGRAPHER
Alexis Xenakis

SECOND PHOTOGRAPHER
Mike Winkleman

DIRECTOR, PUBLISHING
SERVICES
David Xenakis

STYLIST
Rick Mondragon

TECHNICAL ILLUSTRATOR
Carol Skallerud

PRODUCTION DIRECTOR &
COLOR SPECIALIST
Dennis Pearson

BOOK PRODUCTION
MANAGER
Susan Becker

DIGITAL PREPRESS
Everett Baker
Nancy Holzer
Jay Reeve

MIS
Jason Bittner

FIRST PUBLISHED IN USA IN 2005 BY XRX, INC.

ISBN 1-893762-23-8
Produced in Sioux Falls, South Dakota, by XRX, Inc.,
PO Box 1525, Sioux Falls, SD 57101-1525 USA 605.338.2450

a publication of XRX BOOKS

Visit us online at www.knittinguniverse.com

scarves
- a Knitter's dozen

photography by
Alexis Xenakis

v

Welcome

Scarves—those long, skinny rectangles
we love to fling, wrap, knot or not—are
the perfect impulse knits. One piece, the
simplest shape (cast on, knit until it's a scarf,
bind off), and relatively small—scarves are
quick no-brainers. They are also the perfect
accessory—filling in, tieing together, being
seen, and being felt. Their success has been
The Knitting Phenomenon. A ball or two or
three (sometimes scarves aren't that small!) of
something fabulous, a pair of fat needles, and
off we knit. And knit.

Though scarves remain the playground of
knitting, the new game is an interesting
stitch. The novelty is more often an
unfamiliar technique than a fancy yarn. To
join in, find a stitch you like and try it in lots
of different yarns; switch from the finest
mohair to the slinkiest ribbon (that's what
we did with Doin' the Twist). Play with color;
add it by the row, the block, the ruffle. Build
the scarf a stairstep or a short-row wedge
at a time; watch what that does with color!
Drop stitches and chain them up; soon you're
discovering an all-knit, no-loom version of
hairpin lace.

Even sooner your knitter's dozen, like ours, will
grow to twenty-something…or more.

*Throughout this book, the yarns are described generically
and the specific yarn is listed with each photograph. Some
of the yarns are no longer available, but may live on in our
memories and stashes.*

1

Avoid the monotony of garter stitch by adding a little interest. A series of garter ridges is followed by a row containing both a bind-off and a cast-on for a stair-step shape. When worn, the scarf rests on the bias—perfect for any stacking, variegated yarn.

Designed by Knitter's Design Team

Side Steps

Note
See *Techniques*, page 70, for cable cast-on.

Scarf
Cable cast on 16 stitches. * Knit 15 rows.
Next row (RS) Bind off 8 stitches, knit until there are 8 stitches on right needle. Turn work and cable cast on 8 stitches. Repeat from * 14 times more, ending last repeat by binding off all stitches.

EASY

3" x 60"
• approximate finished measurements, from point to point

10cm/4"
32
16

• over garter stitch (knit every row)
• after blocking

1 2 3 **4** 5 6

• Medium weight
• 110 yds

• 5mm/US8, or size to obtain gauge

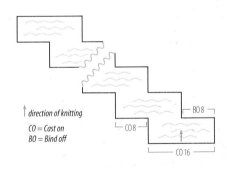

↑ *direction of knitting*

CO = Cast on
BO = Bind off

BO 8
CO 8
CO 16

Scarf NORO Silk Garden (silk, mohair, wool; 50g; 110 yds) in 34
See page 42 for Olive Sash

Hand-dyed colors and fun textures add spark to these simple scarves. They're fun and easy to wear—just lace one end through the slot and forget about it. Knit a bunch in your favorite colors and see how they transform your wardrobe.

Designed by Dana Hurt

Buttonhole Scarf

EASY

SCARVES 1 and 2 • 5" x 65"
SCARF 3 • 6" x 49"
• approximate finished measurements

10cm/4"

• over garter stitch (knit every row) and Stripe Pattern

• Super Bulky weight
SCARF 1 A • 70 yds
SCARF 2 B and C • 70 yds
SCARF 3 A • 90 yds

• Bulky weight
SCARF 1 B and C • 65 yds each
SCARF 2 A • 70 yds
SCARF 3 B AND C • 75 yds

• 8mm/US11, or size to obtain gauge
80cm/32" long

Notes
1 See *Techniques,* page 70, for loop cast-on and making fringe. *2* Knit all rows.

Stripe Pattern 1
Rows 1 and 2 A. *Row 3* B. *Rows 4 and 5* C. *Row 6* B. *Row 7* A. *Row 8* C. *Rows 9 and 10* B. *Row 11* C. *Rows 12–21* Repeat Rows 2-11. *Rows 22–27* Repeat Rows 2-7.

Stripe Pattern 2
Row 1 A. *Row 2* B. *Rows 3 and 4* C. *Row 5* B. *Row 6* A. *Rows 7–24* Repeat Rows 1-6 three times. *Row 25* A. *Row 26* B. *Row 27* C.

Stripe Pattern 3
Rows 1 and 2 A. *Rows 3–5* C. *Rows 6–8* B. *Rows 9–11* A. *Rows 12–29* Repeat Rows 3-11 twice. *Rows 30–35* Repeat Rows 3-8.

SCARVES 1 AND 2
With A, cast on 150 stitches. Work 27 rows in Stripe Pattern 1 or 2, working Rows 8 and 18 as follows: K30, bind off 10 stitches, knit to end. On Rows 9 and 19, loop cast on 10 stitches over bound-off stitches. On Row 28, bind off all stitches loosely with A.

Finishing
Fringe
Cut 14 strands each of A, B, and C, with each strand 24" long. Work fringe along short sides of scarf, using each color 7 times on each side.

SCARF 3
With A, cast on 112 stitches. Work 35 rows in Stripe Pattern 3, working Rows 13 and 23 as follows: K24, bind off 10 stitches, knit to end. On Rows 14 and 24, loop cast on 10 stitches over bound-off stitches. On Row 36, bind off all stitches loosely with A.

Finishing
Fringe
Cut 20 strands each of A, B, and C, with each strand 24" long. Work fringe along short sides of scarf, using each color 10 times on each side.

COLINETTE YARNS
Scarf 3 (on model) Giotto (cotton, rayon, nylon; 100g; 159 yds) in 145 Frangipanni (A); Prism (wool, cotton; 100g; 125 yds) in 110 Autumn Leaves (B); Mohair (mohair, wool, nylon; 100g; 193 yds) in 108 Terracotta (C)

Scarf 1 *Isis in 77 Dusk (A); Prism in 54 Jewel (B) and 134 Jamboree (C)*

Scarf 2 *Prism in 21 Turquoise (A); Isis in 54 Jewel (B); Giotto in 146 Popsicle (C)*

If you choose three colors for a garter stripe scarf, you can easily work one color per row for a wonderful result. It's as easy as braiding hair! Mix it up with textured yarns or rib, seed, or moss stitches.

Designed by Knitter's Design Team

3-Color Garter

Notes

1 Attach color B on Row 2 and color C on Row 3. **2** At the end of each row, drop the color just worked and pick up the next, being careful to always pick up new color in front of the one just dropped.

SCARF

With A, cast on 21 stitches.
Row 1 With B, knit.
Row 2 With C, knit.
Row 3 With A, knit.
Repeat Rows 1–3 until scarf measures 46" from beginning. Bind off.

EASY

6" x 46"
• approximate finished measurements

10cm/4"

26

13

• over garter stitch (knit every row)

1 2 3 4 **5** 6

• Bulky weight
A, B, and C • 65 yds each

• 6.5mm/US10½, or size to obtain gauge

MANOS DEL URUGUAY 100% Wool (100g; 135 yds) in V Cinnamon (A), 111 Blue/Rust/Yellow (B), and W Straw (C)

4

EASY

OLIVE SCARF 3" x 72"
GRAY SCARF 6" x 72"
• approximate finished measurements

10cm/4"
26, 22
18, 14
• over garter stitch (knit every row)

1 2 3 **4 5** 6

• Medium to Bulky weight
A and B • 90 yds each

• two 4.5mm/US7
• two 6.5mm/US10½
or size to obtain gauge

Knit, slide, knit, turn...that's all you do!

Designed by Knitter's Design Team

Sliding Garter

With A, cast on 14 (22) stitches.
Row 1 With B, knit, do not turn work, slide stitches to other end of needle.
Row 2 With A, knit, turn work.
Repeat Rows 1 and 2 until piece measures 72" from beginning. Bind off.

DALE OF NORWAY Sisik (acrylic, mohair, wool, rayon; 50g; 148 yds) in 163 Olive (A) and Heilo (wool; 50g; 110 yds) in 3918 Red (B)

BROWN SHEEP Top of the Lamb (wool; 113g; 180 yds) in Black (A)
CHERRY TREE HILL Thick and Thin (wool, nylon; 227g; 300 yds) in Silver Streak (B)

Here is a great on-the-go project: the shaping and stitch pattern are easy and quick to knit. After the body of the scarf is complete, edge it with a fun, fuzzy, fur-like yarn. Generously sized for evening wear and light as a feather, it could be worn as a chill-chasing shawl as well.

Designed by Terri Shea

Shaped Scarf

EASY +

10½" x 76"
• approximate finished measurements
(including edging)

10cm/4"

32
21

• over Ribbed Garter Pattern
using 3.5mm/US4 needles and MC

1 2 3 **4-5** 6

• Medium weight
MC • 720 yds
• Bulky weight
CC • 131 yds

• 3.5mm/US4, or size to obtain gauge

• 4mm/US6
80cm/32" long

Notes

1 See *Techniques*, page 70, for cable cast-on and pick up and knit. **2** Use cable cast-on throughout. **3** Cast on stitches at end of WS rows only; bind off stitches at beginning of RS rows.

Ribbed Garter Pattern

Row 1 (WS) Knit.
Rows 2 and 4 Knit.
Row 3 * K1, p1; repeat from *. Repeat Rows 1–4 for Ribbed Garter Pattern.

SCARF

With size 3.5mm/US4 needles and MC, cast on 7 stitches.
Begin Ribbed Garter Pattern and cast-on stitches: Row 1 (WS) Knit to end, cast on 5 stitches—12 stitches. Continue in pattern, and, AT SAME TIME, continue to cast on at end of every WS row (working additional stitches into pattern) [3 stitches once, 2 stitches once] 3 times, [1 stitch once, 2 stitches once] 3 times, 1 stitch 3 times—39 stitches, 31 rows total. Cast on 1 stitch at end of every 4th row 4 times—43 stitches, 47 rows total. Cast on 1 stitch at end of every 6th row once,

every 2nd row twice, every 10th row once, every 8th row twice, every 10th row once—50 stitches, 93 rows total. Work even until piece measures 62" from beginning, end with a WS row.
Begin bind-off rows: Row 1 (RS) Bind off 1 stitch, work to end. Continue to bind off 1 stitch every 10th row once, every 8th row twice, every 10th row once—45 stitches, 37 rows. Continue to bind off 1 stitch every 2nd row twice, every 6th row once, every 4th row 4 times, every 2nd row twice—36 stitches, 67 rows. Bind off at beginning of every RS row [2 stitches once, 1 stitch once] 3 times—27 stitches, 79 rows. Then [2 stitches once, 3 stitches once] 3 times—12 stitches, 91 rows.
Row 93 (RS) Bind off 5 stitches, work to end. Bind off remaining 7 stitches.

Finishing

With RS facing, circular needle and CC, begin at cast-on edge and pick up and knit approximately 1 stitch every other row or stitch along shaped edge of scarf. Knit 5 rows. Bind off. Block piece.

AURORA GARNSTUDIO
Karisma (wool; 50g; 120 yds) in Brown (MC) and Pelliza (polyester; 50g; 131 yds) in Brown (CC)

The simplicity of a necktie with the jazz of a fuzzy accent yarn make for a truly fun accessory. This scarf works well wrapped around your neck for warmth, but it's so pretty that you'll want to wear it all day.

Designed by Susan Wills

Bias Scarf

it's easy ...go for it!

EASY

SCARF A 4½" x 64"
SCARF B 3" x 45"
• approximate finished measurements

10cm/4"

26
18
• over stockinette stitch
(knit on RS, purl on WS) using MC

1 2 3 **4** 5 6
• Medium weight
SCARF A MC • 196 yds
SCARF B MC • 120 yd

1 2 3 4 **5** 6
• Bulky weight
SCARF A CC • 40 yds
SCARF B CC • 60 yds

• 5mm/US8
or size to obtain gauge

Note
See *Techniques*, page 70, for knit into front and back (kf&b).

Bias Garter Pattern A
Rows 1, 3, 5, 7, 9, 11, and 13 (RS) With MC, kf&b of first stitch, knit to last 2 sts, k2tog.
Rows 2 and 10 Purl.
Rows 4, 6, 8, 12, and 14 Knit.
Row 15 With CC, kf&b of first stitch, knit to last 2 sts, k2tog.
Row 16 With CC, knit.
Rows 17–32 Repeat Rows 1–8 twice.
Rows 33–40 Repeat Rows 9–16 once.
Repeat Rows 1–40 for Bias Garter Pattern A.

Bias Garter Pattern B
RS rows Kf&b of first stitch, knit to last 2 stitches, k2tog.
WS rows Knit.

SCARF A
With MC, cast on 30 stitches. Work Rows 1–40 of Bias Garter Pattern A 8 times, then work Rows 1–10 once more. Piece measures approximately 64" from beginning. Bind off.

SCARF B
With CC, cast on 20 stitches. Work Bias Garter Pattern B as follows: * 2 rows with CC, 6 rows with MC; repeat from * until scarf measures approximately 45" from beginning, ending with 2 rows CC. Bind off with CC.

Scarf A on page 14 Original yarns KARABELLA YARNS Aurora 8 (wool; 50g; 98 yds) in 1145 Dark Green (MC) and Butterfly (rayon; 50g; 40 yds) in 65 (CC)

Scarf B PLYMOUTH YARNS Galway (wool; 100g; 210 yds) in 9 Black (MC) and Hot! Hot! Hot! (nylon, polyester, acrylic; 50g; 33 yds) in 692 Multicolor (CC)

7

A scarf is the perfect opportunity to take advantage of the color repeats in handpaint yarns. Watch the magic happen as colors stack and flow when you work a bias lace pattern in garter.

Designed by Knitter's Design Team

Color Shift

it's
easy
...go
for it!

EASY+

6" x 68"
• approximate finished measurements

10cm/4"

15
12
• over Lace Pattern
• after blocking

1 2 3 **4** 5 6

• Medium weight
• 240 yds

• 6mm/US10, or size to obtain gauge

Lace Pattern (over an even number of stitches)
Row 1 (RS) K3, yo, * k2tog, yo; repeat from * to last 3 stitches, k3.
Row 2 (WS) K2, k2tog, knit to end.
Repeat Rows 1 and 2 for Lace Pattern.

SCARF
Cast on 24 stitches.
Knit 3 rows.
Work Lace Pattern until piece measures 67" from beginning, ending with a WS row.
Knit 4 rows. Bind off.

FIESTA La Boheme (1-strand mohair blend,
1 strand rayon bouclé; 4 oz; 145 yds) in color Adirondack

EASY +

HORIZONTAL SCARF • 7" x 60"
VERTICAL SCARF • 5" x 60"
•approximate finished measurements

10cm/4"

22, 32
10, 20

• over seed stitch with 3 strands held together
• over garter stitch (knit every row)

1 2 3 **4 5** 6

• Medium–Bulky weight
A, B, & C • 190 yds
• 175 yds

• 8mm/US11
• 5mm/US8
or size to obtain gauge

&

• Waste yarn

A little knitting goes a long way when you drop stitches—deliberately and skillfully. The resulting ladders offer graceful motion and additional length or width depending on how you orient your knitting.

Designed by Knitter's Design Team

Waterfall Scarf

Note
See *Techniques*, page 70, for knit, purl through back loop (tbl).

Seed Stitch (over an odd number of stitches)
* K1, p1; repeat from *, end k1.

HORIZONTAL SCARF
With waste yarn, cast on 89 sts. Knit 2 rows. Change to A, B, and C held together.
Row 1 (RS) * K1, p1; repeat from * to end.
Row 2 only * P1 through back loop (tbl), k1 tbl; repeat from * to end.
Work in seed stitch until piece measures 7" from beginning. Bind off in Waterfall bind-off.
Finishing
Remove waste yarn. Block piece.

VERTICAL SCARF
With waste yarn, cast on 19 sts. Knit 2 rows. Change to MC.
Row 1 (RS) Knit.
Row 2 only Knit into back of every stitch.
Knit every row for approximately 53".
Bind off in Waterfall bind-off.
Finishing
Remove waste yarn. Block piece.

Waterfall bind-off

1 Bind off 4 sts in pattern, * remove loop from right needle and pull skein of yarn through loop.

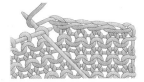

2 Work next 2 stitches. Repeat Steps 1 and 2 across piece.

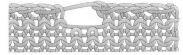

Bind off remaining stitches, fasten off.
3 Remove needle, drop the paired stitches down to the cast-on edge, forming ladders.

Vertical Scarf, on page 20 SKACEL
  Unikat (wool; 100g; 176 yds) in 04

Horizontal Scarf BLUE HERON YARNS
Silk/Rayon Twist (225g; 350 yds) in Dusk (A)
Cotton/Rayon Seed (225g; 490 yds) in Dusk (B)
Confetti (poly/acrylic; 90g; 425 yds) in Dusk (C)

Always
Open

9

Play with color and technique. Take neon brights and work stair-step intarsia blocks in garter. Rather than worry about neat color joins, leave them out for decorative holes that will always remain open.

Designed by Knitter's Design Team

Always Open

INTERMEDIATE

4½" x 66"
• approximate finished size

10cm/4"

34
24

• garter stitch (knit every row)

1 **2** 3 4 5 6

• Fine weight
A • 40 yds
B, C, and F • 75 yds
D • 60 yds
E • 65 yds

• 3.5mm/US4, or size to obtain gauge

Visit
www.knittinguniverse.com
to design your own color scheme with
Knitter's Paintbox.

Notes
1 Break yarn between color stripes and blocks and weave in colors as you go.
2 To eliminate the floats at the stairsteps, knit the second and fourth stitches of C2 under the float at each step.

Block Pattern (over 25 stitches)
Note Do not twist yarns together at color change.
Rows 1–6 With first color (C1), knit.
Row 7 (RS) With C1, k20, then with 2nd color (C2), k5.
Row 8 With C2, k5; with C1, k20.
Rows 9–12 Repeat Rows 7 and 8 twice.
Row 13 With C1, k15; with C2, k10.
Row 14 With C2, k10; with C1, k15.
Rows 15–18 Repeat Rows 13 and 14 twice.
Row 19 With C1, k10; with C2, k15.
Row 20 With C2, k15; with C1, k10.
Rows 21–24 Repeat Rows 19 and 20 twice.
Row 25 With C1, k5; with C2, k20.
Row 26 With C2, k20; with C1, k5.
Row 27–30 Repeat Rows 25 and 26 twice.
Row 31–36 With C2, knit.

SCARF
With A, cast on 25 stitches.
Begin color sequence: Knit 5 rows, ending with a WS row. Change to B. Knit 6 rows. Work 2 more 6-row stripes with colors shown on Color Sequence Diagram. Work 36-row Block pattern with E as C1 and F as C2. Continue working Block patterns and color stripes, following Color Sequence Diagram. After last stripe, bind off.

Block Pattern

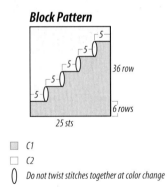

□ C1
□ C2
() Do not twist stitches together at color change

DALE OF NORWAY Falk (wool; 50g; 116 yds) in 7081 Charcoal (A), 0144 Pink (B), 0184 Green (C), 0138 Red (D), 0120 Yellow (E), and 0130 Orange (F)

Color Sequence

- ■ A
- ■ B
- □ C
- ■ D
- □ E
- ■ F

The classics take on new life when you combine garter stitch with tubular knitting. Thanks to this combination, the bowtie and necktie shaping is organic.

Designed by Knitter's Design Team

Black Tie Optional

Notes
1 See *Techniques*, page 70, for SSK. **2** Slip stitches purlwise with yarn in front. **3** The length of the bowtie is adjustable. Use a cabone ring to adjust and refine fit, when necessary.

BOWTIE (MAKE 2)
Cast on 12 stitches.
Rows 1–15 Knit.
Rows 16–29 * K1, slip 1; repeat from * to end. Knit 32 rows.
Band
Next row * K1, slip 1; repeat from * to end. Repeat last row until band measures length to center back neck plus 1", then SSK or k2tog across next row—6 stitches. Work 5 rows in stockinette stitch (knit one row, purl one row). Bind off.

Assembly
Thread one band through a cabone ring, fold back 1", and sew to secure. Repeat for second half but temporarily secure with safety pin. Try on and tie the bow. Adjust fit by repositioning safety pin as necessary, untie bow then secure second band.

NECKTIE
Cast on 16 stitches.
Rows 1–13 Knit.
Rows 14–27 * K1, slip 1; repeat from * to end.
Rows 28–41 Knit. [Repeat Rows 14–41] 13 times. Bind off.

Bowtie *BERROCO Suede (nylon; 50g; 120 yds) in 3704 Wrangler*

Assembly

EASY

BOWTIE • 30½"
NECKTIE • 48"
• approximate finished length

10cm/4"

32
22
• over garter stitch (knit every row)

 1 2 3 **4** 5 6

• Medium weight
BOWTIE • 72 yds
NECKTIE • 150 yds

• 4mm/US6, or size to obtain gauge

&

• 1" cabone ring for joining bowtie

Tying a Four-in-Hand Knot

1 With shorter length
of tie in front . . .

2 . . . wrap longer length
around front and
under loop at neck.

3 Pull through loop
and neaten.

Necktie TRENDSETTER *Diamante*
(viscose, nylon; 50g; 120 yds) in 14

Tying a Bowtie

If you can tie a square knot, you can tie a bowtie! Practice with a length of ribbon.

2 *Take bow in right hand and tuck under left bow, let it fall to front.*

4 *Take back portion and form half bow, placing fold at left side of body.*

6 *Adjust by holding folds of tail.*

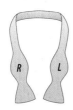

1 *Place tie around neck.*

3 *Adjust, with extra length on front bow.*

5 *Fold front bow, take fold behind loop of first bow, and tuck it through knot.*

Bridge
the Gap 11

This scarf is knit lengthwise, but ever so simply—separate blocks are joined together by subsequent ones. The sequence is logical and practical. You can't help but fall in love with the ease and versatility of the process, and you can decide when it is done—after 9 repeats, maybe 12, or even 15.

Designed by Knitter's Design Team

Bridge the Gap

INTERMEDIATE

4½" x 80"
• approximate finished measurements

10cm/4"

32 16
• over garter stitch (knit every row)

1 2 3 **4** 5 6

• Medium weight
A-E • 65 yds each

• 5mm/US8, or size to obtain gauge

Visit
www.knittinguniverse.com
to design your own color scheme with
Knitter's Paintbox.

Notes

1 See *Techniques*, page 70, for slipping stitches. **2** Follow Color Placement diagram for color of each block. **3** Build blocks diagonally across the scarf. This requires putting stitches on hold. **4** Slip all stitches purlwise.

Base Block

With desired color, cast on 16 sts. Knit 13 rows, ending with a WS row (mark RS of work). Break yarn.

Half Block

With RS facing and next color, knit 8 stitches from Base Block. Knit 13 more rows on these 8 stitches. Break yarn.

Bridge Block

With RS facing and next color, knit 16 (last 8 stitches from first Block and first 8 stitches from second Block); turn work. Knit 13 more rows on these 16 stitches.

SCARF

Block 1 Work a Base Block. Turn work.
Block 2 Work a Half Block. Turn work and slip stitches of all blocks to right needle.
*** Block 3** Cast on 16 stitches onto right needle and work a new Base Block, then slip 8 stitches of previous Base Block to right needle, turn work.
Block 4 Work a Bridge Block. Break yarn, then with WS facing slip all stitches to right needle and turn work.
Block 5 Work Bridge Block. Turn work and bind off 16 stitches, then break yarn and fasten off. With RS facing, slip all stitches to right needle.
Repeat from * to desired length, then work a Half Block over last stitches of Base Block, ending with Bridge Block. Bind off.

HARRISVILLE Orchid (wool, mohair, silk; 100g; 245 yds) in 232 Purple Quartz (A), 231 Raspberry (B), 236 Sunflower (C), 239 Clay (D), and 240 Willow (E)

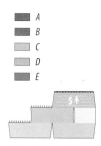

	A
	B
	C
	D
	E

Bridge Block with bind-off

Bridge Block

Base Block

Half Block

Base Block

Color Placement

29

12

This is a variation of the hairpin lace pattern popular in crochet. We make it simple by eliminating the pin or fork and even the hook. All we need is a pair of knitting needles and our fingers. The best part is that any reversible stitch will work, with as many strips as you choose.

Designed by Rick Mondragon

Do-be-do

EASY+

SCARVES A & B • 5" x 48, 58"
SCARVES C & D • 6" x 72"

10cm/4"

20, 18, 22, 15

18, 16, 18, 15

SCARVES A, B, C• over garter stitch
(knit every row)
SCARF D • over seed stitch

1 2 3-4-5 6

• Light weight
(yarn used double strand)
SCARF A • 285 yds
• Medium weight
SCARF C • 140 yds MC
SCARF C • 70 yds CC
SCARF D • 175 yds
• Bulky Weight
SCARF B • 125 yds

SCARF A • 5mm/US8
SCARVES B, C, D • 8mm/US11
or size to obtain gauge

Notes

1 Each scarf is made of strips that are connected with loops made from dropped stitches. These loops can be connected by using a crochet hook or your fingers. **2** Mark right side (RS) of each strip. **3** See scarf instructions for required number of stitches to cast on and rows to work.

Garter Stitch Pattern
All rows Knit.

Seed Stitch Pattern (over an odd number of stitches)
All rows * K1, p1; repeat from *, end k1.

Strips

Cast on required number of stitches. Work required number of rows, ending with a RS row. Leave on double-pointed needle (dpn). Cut yarn, leaving a 30" tail.

SCARF A

Working with 2 strands held together, work two 10-stitch strips in garter stitch, 287 rows each.

SCARF B

Work one 10-stitch strip and one 5-stitch strip, both in garter stitch and 287 rows.

SCARF C

Work 3 strips: two 12-stitch strips in MC and one in CC, all in garter stitch and 431 rows.

SCARF D

Work two 5-stitch strips and one 11-stitch strip, all in seed stitch and 359 rows.

Assembly
SCARVES A AND B

Drop last 2 stitches of 10-stitch strip (right strip) and first 2 stitches of second strip (left strip; for scarf B, this is a 5-stitch strip). Join strips.
SCARF C

Drop last 2 stitches of one MC strip (right strip) and first 2 stitches of other MC strip (left strip). Drop first and last 2 stitches of CC strip (center strip). Join strips.
SCARF D

Drop last 2 stitches of one 5-stitch strip (right strip) and first 2 stitches of other 5-stitch strip (left strip). Drop first and last 2 stitches of 11-stitch strip (center strip). Join strips.

JOIN STRIPS

Ravel the dropped stitches back to cast-on edge. Place strips side by side.

Beginning at bottom of strips and following illustrations, join loops formed by dropped stitches. (For Scarf A, 2 loops = 4 strands.)

Joining Strips

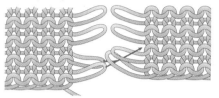

1 * Pull 2 loops from left through 2 loops from right.

2 Pull next 2 loops from right through left loops. Repeat from * until all loops are chained together.

3 Pull 30" tail from right strip through last 2 loops of left strip, leaving enough slack to create a loop, and bind off across the right strip. Bind off left strip.

Scarf A on page 34, left ELLEN'S HALF-PINT FARM Silk and Merino-W (500g; 1370 yds) in Mexican Siesta; yarn used double
Scarf B on page 31 SKACEL Unikat (wool; 100g; 176 yds) in 04
Scarf C on pages 30 and 34, right MUENCH String of Pearls (cotton, viscose, polyester; 50g; 99 yds) in 4013 (MC); TRENDSETTER Pepita (polyamid, polyester; 50g; 95 yds) in 188 (CC)
Scarf D MANETTO HILL YARNERY Luxura (cashmere; 100g; 186 yds) in 61214

Even though you may never samba at Carnival in Rio, your needles can dance as you knit a scarf inspired by Carmen Miranda. The knitting maneuvers are not difficult—just slip-stitch knitting and yarn-over increases.

Designed by Rick Mondragon

Carmen

EASY+

5" x 48"
· approximate finished measurements with ruffles attached

10cm/4"

26

20

· over Slip-Stitch Ridge Pattern

1 2 **3** 4 5 6

· Light weight
MC · 123 yds
A, B, D, E · 55 yds each
C · 65 yds
F, G, H, I, J, K · 45 yds each

· 4.5mm/US7, or size to obtain gauge
60cm/24" long,

Visit
www.knittinguniverse.com
to design your own color scheme with
Knitter's Paintbox.

Notes

1 See *Techniques*, page 70, for cable cast-on and yarn over. *2* Pick up stitches for ruffles with RS of body facing and along slip-stitch ridges, follow diagram for placement of color and long or short ruffles.

Slip-Stitch Ridge Pattern (multiple of 5 + 1)

Row 1 (RS) * K1, p4; repeat from *, end k1.
Row 2 (WS) * Slip 1, k4; repeat from *, end slip 1.

Body

With MC and cable cast-on, cast on 21 stitches. Work 250 rows in Slip-Stitch Ridge Pattern, ending with Row 2. Bind off.

Ruffles

Work Ruffles following Ruffle Color Placement diagram.

Long Ruffle

Row 1 Pick up and k1, [yo, pick up and k1] 24 times—49 sts.
Row 2 and all even rows Knit.
Row 3 [K2, yo] 24 times, end k1—73 sts.
Row 5 [K3, yo] 24 times, end k1—97 sts.
Row 7 [K4, yo] 24 times, end k1—121 sts.
Row 8 Knit.
Bind off.

Short Ruffle (worked at beginning of tier)

Row 1 Pick up and k1, [yo, pick up and k1] 12 times—25 sts.
Row 2 and all even rows Knit.
Row 3 [K2, yo] 12 times, end k1—37 sts.
Row 5 [K3, yo] 12 times, end k1—49 sts.
Row 7 [K4, yo] 12 times, end k1—61 sts.
Row 8 Knit.
Bind off.

Short Ruffle (worked at end of tier)

Row 1 Pick up and k1, [yo, pick up and k1] 11 times—23 sts.
Row 2 and all even rows Knit.
Row 3 [K2, yo] 11 times, end k1—34 sts.
Row 5 [K3, yo] 11 times, end k1—45 sts.
Row 7 [K4, yo] 11 times, end k1—56 sts.
Row 8 Knit.
Bind off.

Finishing

To block scarf, wash according to yarn manufacturers instructions. Lay flat allowing ruffles to fall across one another at random.

ROWAN YARNS
Yorkshire Tweed DK (wool; 50g; 123 yds) in 349 Frog (MC), 348 Lime Leaf (A), and 344 Scarlet (E); Felted Tweed (wool, alpaca, viscose; 50g; 191 yds) in 146 Herb (B), 154 Pickle (F), 155 Ginger (H), and 152 Watery (I); Rowanspun DK (wool; 50g; 219 yds) in 731 Punch (C), 735 Eau de Nil (D), 736 Goblin (G), 734 Cloud (J), and 747 Catkin (K)

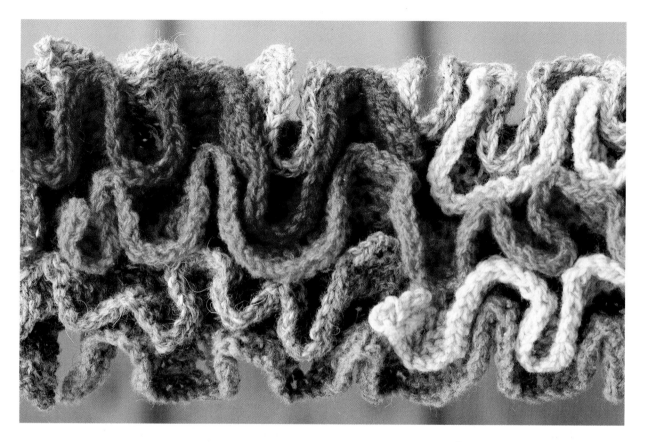

Ruffle Color Placement

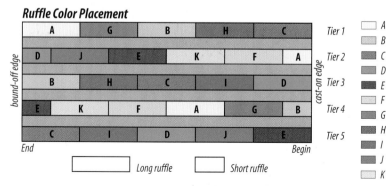

A		G	B	H		C	Tier 1
D	J		E	K	F	A	Tier 2
B		H	C	I		D	Tier 3
E	K		F	A	G	B	Tier 4
	C	I	D	J		E	Tier 5

bound-off edge ... *cast-on edge*

End ... Begin

Long ruffle   Short ruffle

- A
- B
- C
- D
- E
- F
- G
- H
- I
- J
- K

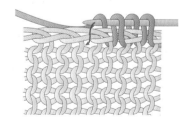

Pick up stitches for ruffles along slip-stitch ridges working a yarn over between each picked-up stitch.

Sock
Scarf

How about a scarf that employs sock techniques? We took total advantage of the stacking yarns by knitting a tube and adding afterthought heels every few inches. We chose to stagger them so the scarf would not lie flat, no matter how you wear it.

Designed by Robyn Hamilton

Sock Scarf

INTERMEDIATE

3¼" x 76"
• approximate finished measurements

10cm/4"

23 | 19

• over stockinette stitch (knit every round)

 1 2 3 **4** 5 6

• Medium weight
• 450 yds

• 5mm/US8 double-pointed needles (dpn)
or size to obtain gauge

• 5mm/H-8

&

• contrasting color waste yarn

Notes

1 See *Techniques,* page 70, for SSK, chain cast-on, and stockinette stitch grafting. **2** Scarf is worked in a tube and heels are worked later.

SCARF

Chain cast on 36 stitches divided evenly over 3 dpns—12/12/12. Join, being careful not to twist stitches. Knit 34 rounds. * With waste yarn, k18, turn work and p18, turn work. With working yarn, knit 34 rounds. After last round has been worked, knit an additional 9 stitches for new end of round. Repeat from * 10 times more, omitting the additional 9 stitches the last time. Redistribute stitches, if necessary, so that stitches are evenly divided over 3 dpns.

Shape toe

Needle 1 K9, slip remaining 3 stitches to next needle to the left; **Needle 2** K9, slip remaining 6 stitches to next needle to the left; **Needle 3** K18—9/9/18. **Begin decreases: Round 1** SSK, knit to end of Needle 1; knit to last 2 stitches of Needle 2, k2tog; on Needle 3, SSK, knit to last 2 stitches, k2tog. **Round 2** Knit. Repeat Rounds 1 and 2 three times more. Repeat Round 1 twice more—12 stitches. Slip 3 stitches from one needle onto the other with 3 stitches. Graft 6 stitches from each needle together.

Heels

Remove waste yarn, placing 18 stitches at top and bottom each on a needle. With RS facing, pick up and knit 1 stitch between the 2 rows at end of needles, k9 (Needle 1), k9 onto another needle (Needle 2), then with another needle, pick up and knit 1 stitch between 2 rows, then k18 (Needle 3). Repeat decrease rounds 1 and 2 as for toe until there are 14 stitches. Slip 3 stitches from one needle onto the one with 4 stitches. Graft 7 stitches from each needle together. Work heel at each waste yarn row.

Shape 2nd toe

Remove waste yarn from cast-on edge, and divide stitches over 3 dpns—12/12/12. Join yarn and knit 1 round. Work as for first toe.

SCHOELLER/STAHL Big Mexiko (superwash wool; 50g; 93 yds) in 7952 Sundown

Doin'
the
Twist

15

15

Mary Thomas' Elongated Crossed Garter Stitch takes on a new look when worked in wide ribbon. We have even updated the maneuver, just wrap the crossed needles and knit through the wrap and stitch–for a scarf that knits up quickly and beautifully.

Designed by Knitter's Design Team

Doin' the Twist

EASY

SCARF A • 3" x 96"
SASH (SCARF) B • 1½" (8") x 50" (60")
SCARF C • 6" x 70"
• approximate finished measurements

10cm/4"

6, 13 (14), 6
10, 18 (21), 10
• over Twist Pattern
• over Garter Twist Pattern
• over Sliding Twist Pattern

1 2 3 **4** 5 **6**
• Medium weight
• 70 (180) yds
CC • 50 yds
• Super Bulky weight
• 260 yds
MC • 120 yds

• 8mm/US11
• 4.5mm/US7
or size to obtain gauge

• set of two 8mm/US11

&

6mm beads (optional)

42

Note
See *Techniques*, page 70, for cable cast-on, making fringe and adding beads.

Twist Pattern
Work Twist stitch every row.

Garter Twist Pattern
Row 1 Work Twist stitch.
Row 2 Knit.
Repeat Rows 1 and 2 for Garter Twist Pattern.

Sliding Twist Pattern
Row 1 With CC, knit across, do not turn, slide stitches to other side of needle.
Row 2 With MC, work Twist stitch across, turn work.
Repeat Rows 1 and 2 for Sliding Twist Pattern.

SCARF A
Cast on 9 stitches. Work in Twist Pattern until piece measures 90" or desired length from beginning, end with a WS row. Bind off.

SASH (SCARF) B
Cast on 8 (30) sts, work Garter Twist Pattern until piece measures 50" (60") or desired length.

Optional beaded fringe for sash: 1 Cut 28, 10" lengths. **2** Attach fringe in space between stitches at each end of sash. **3** Add beads and knot.

SCARF C
With double-pointed needles and MC, cable cast on 15 stitches. Work in Sliding Twist Pattern until piece measures 45" or desired length.
Bind off.

Fringe
Cut 30, 14" lengths of MC and attach to ends of scarf.

Scarf A on page 41 TRENDSETTER Segue (nylon; 50g; 120 yds) in 1337
Sash B on page 3 BERROCO Suede (nylon; 50g; 120 yds) in 3715 Tonto or 3757 Clementine
Scarf B on page 44 MADIL Kid Seta (mohair, silk; 25g; 230 yds) in 830
Scarf C TRENDSETTER Segue (nylon; 50g; 120 yds) in 1341 (MC) and
MANOS DEL URUGUAY 100% Wool (wool; 100g; 138yds) in Yellow (CC)

Twist stitch

1 Place right needle into stitch.

2 Wrap yarn around both needle tips.

3 Then wrap yarn around right needle.

4 Draw yarn through the first wrap and stitch.

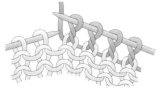

5 Drop wrap and stitch from left needle.

16
Pocket
Scarf

Comfortable and versatile as a favorite pair of jeans, you can throw on this pocket scarf and happily ward off the winter chill in style. The pockets are large enough for easy access to your cell phone or keys when you're dashing about. The accent is woven in, for additional interest.

Designed by Lily M. Chin

Pocket Scarf

INTERMEDIATE +

10" x 65"
• approximate finished measurements

10cm/4"

30

23
• over Chart B using MC

1 2 **3** 4 5 6

Light weight
MC • 640 yds

1 2 3 **4** 5 6

• Medium weight
CC • 96 yds

• 3.75mm/US5
or size to obtain gauge

SCARF

With MC, cast on 57 stitches. Join CC and work as follows:

Begin Chart A: Row 1 (RS) Slip 1 (sl 1) purlwise with yarn in back (wyib), bring CC to WS (if it's not there already), bring MC to RS and p1MC, * bring CC to RS, MC to WS and k2MC, bring CC to WS, MC to RS and p1MC; repeat from * to last stitch, bring CC to RS, MC to WS and k1MC.

Row 2 Sl 1 purlwise with yarn in front (wyif), * bring CC to WS, MC to RS and k1MC, bring CC to RS, MC to WS and p2MC; repeat from * to last 2 stitches, bring CC to WS, MC to RS and k1MC, bring CC to RS, MC to WS and p1MC.

Row 3 Repeat Row 1.

Row 4 (Yarns are already in correct place to start row.) Sl 1 wyif, * p2MC, bring CC to WS, MC to RS and k3MC, bring CC to RS, MC to WS, p1MC; repeat from * to last 2 stitches, p1MC, bring CC to WS, p1MC. Continue in pattern as established through chart row 23. Cut CC. Continue with MC only.

Begin Chart B: Row 1 (WS) Sl 1 wyif, * p2, k3, p1; repeat from * to last 2 stitches, p2.

Row 2 Sl 1 wyib, k1, * k1, p3, k2; repeat from * to last stitch, k1. Continue in chart pattern until piece measures approximately 61" from beginning, ending with chart row 17. Join CC and work 23 rows of Chart A. Bind off.

Top Pocket

With MC, cast on 33 stitches. Begin with a WS row, work 13 rows of Chart C. Cut CC. With MC only, work Rows 6-20 of Chart B, then work Rows 1-17 once more. Bind off.

Lower Pocket

With MC, cast on 33 stitches. Begin with a WS row, work Rows 1-20 of Chart B, then work Rows 1-12 once more. Join CC and work 13 rows of Chart C. Bind off.

Finishing

Block pieces. Sew pockets to scarf, centered and abutting scarf borders.

SKACEL Samo (kid mohair, cotton, acrylic, wool; 25g; 80 yds) in Denim (MC) and Stahl Wolle Flanell (merino, acrylic; 50g; 96 yds) in Flag Blue (CC)

Chart B

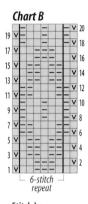

6-stitch repeat

Stitch key for Chart B

K on RS, p on WS
P on RS, k on WS
Sl 1 purlwise with yarn at WS

Chart A

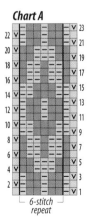

6-stitch repeat

Chart C

6-stitch repeat

Stitch key for Charts A & C

On RS rows

Bring CC to opposite side of work, bring MC to WS and k with MC
Bring CC to WS, MC to RS and p with MC
Bring CC to RS, MC to WS and k with MC
Sl 1 purlwise with yarn in back (wyib)

On WS rows

Bring CC to opposite side of work, bring MC to WS and p with MC
Bring CC to WS, MC to RS and k with MC
Bring CC to RS, MC to WS and p with MC
Sl 1 purlwise with yarn in front (wyif)

 RS
 RS
 WS
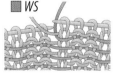 WS

Even knitters who are new to Aran patterns can create a rich design. A luxurious cashmere and silk yarn is knit into a scarf where the cables seem to dance across the handpainted color.

Designed by Jean Schafer-Albers

Cables In Cashmere

INTERMEDIATE

7" x 47½"
• approximate finished measurements

10cm/4"

38
27
• over stockinette stitch
(knit on RS, purl on WS)

1 2 **3** 4 5 6
• Light weight
• 380 yds

• 3.5mm/US4, or size to obtain gauge

&
• cable needle (cn)

Note
See *Techniques*, page 70, for binding off in pattern.

Seed Stitch Pattern
Over an even number of stitches
Row 1 (RS) * K1, p1; repeat from *.
Row 2 * P1, k1; repeat from *.
Repeat Rows 1 and 2 for Seed stitch.

SCARF
Cast on 60 stitches.
Foundation row (WS) [P1, k1] twice, k2, p8, k2, [p1, k1] twice, k2, p3, k10, p3, k2, [p1, k1] twice, k2, p8, k2, [p1, k1] twice.
Begin Charts A, B, C, and seed stitch:
Row 1 (RS) Work 4 stitches seed stitch, 12 stitches Chart A, 4 stitches seed stitch, 20 stitches Chart B, 4 stitches seed stitch, 12 stitches Chart C, 4 stitches seed stitch. Continue in patterns as established until piece measures 47½" from beginning, ending with Row 24 of Chart B. Bind off in pattern.

Finishing
Block piece.

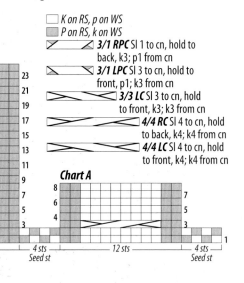

☐ K on RS, p on WS
▨ P on RS, k on WS
3/1 RPC Sl 1 to cn, hold to back, k3; p1 from cn
3/1 LPC Sl 3 to cn, hold to front, p1; k3 from cn
3/3 LC Sl 3 to cn, hold to front, k3; k3 from cn
4/4 RC Sl 4 to cn, hold to back, k4; k4 from cn
4/4 LC Sl 4 to cn, hold to front, k4; k4 from cn

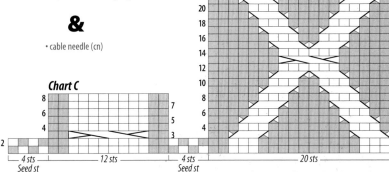

Chart B

Chart C

Chart A

4 sts Seed st | 12 sts | 4 sts Seed st | 20 sts | 4 sts Seed st | 12 sts | 4 sts Seed st

48

Original yarn CHERRY TREE HILL Cashmere and Silk (cashmere, silk; 50g; 228 yds) in Martha's Vineyard

A simple wedge of 12 or 16 short rows sends your knitting off in a new direction. Use the wedges in multiples for a U-turn curve, or separate them with an odd number of complete rows to form a wave design, just experiment with different combinations. This knitting's fun, as it should be.

Designed by Patricia Kalthoff

Wavy Scarves

EASY +

SCARF A • 4" x 62"
SCARF B • 9" x 68"
SCARF C • 9" x 70" (red)
4" x 66" (aqua)
• approximate finished measurements

10cm/4"
15 (A, C)
17 (B)
8 (A, C);
11 (B)
• over garter stitch (knit every row)

1 2 3 **4** 5 **6**

• Medium weight
SCARF A • 228 yds
SCARF C • 210 yds
• Super Bulky weight
SCARF B • 370 yds

SCARVES A & C
• 4.5mm/US7
SCARF B
• 10mm/US15
or size to obtain gauge

Notes
1 See *Techniques*, page 70, for wrap and turn for short rows (W&T). **2** On the scarf diagrams, the numbers indicate the number of complete knit rows worked between short-row wedges.

Short-row Wedge
A wedge is created by working progressively shorter rows every odd-numbered row, then working the last 2 rows over all stitches. Begin the wedge on either a RS or WS row, depending on the shape desired.

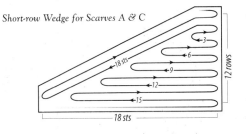

Short-row Wedge for Scarves A & C

18 sts

18 sts

12 rows

←3
←6
←9
←12
←15

Short-row Wedge for Scarves A & C
Row 1 K15, W&T.
Row 2 and all even-numbered rows Knit to end.
Row 3 K12, W&T.
Row 5 K9, W&T.
Row 7 K6, W&T.
Row 9 K3, W&T.
Rows 11 and 12 K18.

Scarf A MOUNTAIN COLORS *Merino Ribbon (wool; 100g; 245 yds) in Sagebrush*
Scarf C on page 51 NORO *Silk Garden (silk, mohair, wool; 50g; 109 yds) in 86*

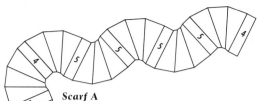

Scarf A
A combination of Scarves B and C.

SCARF A

Cast on 18 stitches. Knit 6 rows.
* [Work Short-row Wedge] 3 times, knit
5 rows; repeat from * 3 times more.
[Work Short-row Wedge] 3 times, knit
4 rows.
*[Work Short-row Wedge] 3 times,
knit 5 rows; repeat from * 4 times
more, ending last repeat knit 4 rows.
Bind off.

Scarf B Original yarn
TAHKI·STACY CHARLES Magic
(merino wool; 50g; 74 yds) in 02

Scarf B

*Four short-row wedges are
placed on each side of a center
rectangle (worked on an even
number of stitches), creating
an arch.*

Short-row Wedge for Scarf B

Row 1 K21, W&T.
Row 2 *and all even-numbered rows* Knit to end.
Row 3 K18, W&T.
Row 5 K15, W&T.
Row 7 K12, W&T.
Row 9 K9, W&T.
Row 11 K6, W&T.
Row 13 K3, W&T.
Rows 15 and 16 K24.

Short-row Wedge for Scarf B

SCARF B

(For a neater edge, slip first stitch of every
row purlwise with yarn in front.) Cast on
24 stitches. Knit 136 rows. [Work Short-row
Wedge] 4 times. Knit 8 rows. [Work Short-row
Wedge] 4 times. Knit 134 rows. Bind off.

Scarf C

Three short-row wedges worked from one direction are stacked on top of three short-row wedges worked from the opposite direction.

SCARF C

Cast on 18 stitches. Knit 6 rows. *[Work Short-row Wedge] 3 times, knit 5 rows; repeat from* 6 times more, ending last repeat knit 6 rows.

Scarf C *Oringinal yarn TAHKI•STACY CHARLES Cozy (wool, nylon; 50g; 42 yds) in 4 Orange*

19

This lace was inspired by motifs on Native American baskets. The scarf begins in the center and is worked to each end. The thunderbird pattern is bordered by a feather design at the ends and eyelets at the sides. Done in a cushy, soft merino, the scarf has a masculine appeal; for a more feminine look, use the feather pattern (Chart C) and 40-row T-bird lace (Chart B) along the full length of the scarf.

Designed by Evelyn Clark

T-Bird Scarf

INTERMEDIATE

7" x 51"
• approximate finished measurement

10cm/4"
31
18
• over garter stitch (knit every row)

1 2 3 **4** 5 6

• Medium weight
• 396 yds

• 4.5mm/US7
or size to obtain gauge

Notes

1 See *Techniques*, page 70, for SSK, SK2P, and invisible cast-on. **2** Scarf is knit in 2 sections from center out to each end. **3** For ease in working, mark right side of work.

SCARF

Invisibly cast on 33 stitches. Work Rows 1–4 of Chart A 35 times, then work Rows 5–6 once. * Work 40 rows of Chart B. Work Rows 1–4 of Chart C twice, then work Rows 5–6 once. Knit 3 rows. Bind off knitwise.*

Second half

Remove waste yarn from cast-on stitches and place 33 stitches on needle, ready to work a wrong-side row. Join yarn and work Rows 2–4 of Chart A once, work Rows 1–4 of Chart A 34 times, then work Rows 5–6 once. Work from * to * of first half.

Finishing

Block piece.

Chart C

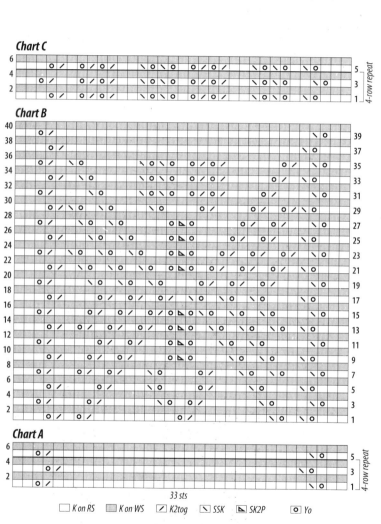

Chart B

Chart A

33 sts

□ K on RS ▨ K on WS ╱ K2tog ╲ SSK ◣ SK2P ⊙ Yo

NEEDFUL YARNS King Extra (merino wool; 50g; 99 yds) in Gray

55

What's your fancy? Make this same design using two weights of the same wool to create two different sizes and looks. Mary Kay gives us a special design straight from the Shetland Isles.

Designed by Mary Kay

Shetland Lace

INTERMEDIATE +

1-PLY SCARF" • 8½" x 34"
2-PLY SCARF • 11" x 44"
• approximate finished measurements

10cm/4"

56, 36

32, 24

• over chart rows 8–23 (16-row repeat)

 2 3 4 5 6

• Super Fine weight
• 1-PLY COBWEB 430 yds
• 2-PLY LACE WEIGHT 500 yds

• 2.75mm/US2
• 3.25mm/US3
or size to obtain gauge

• stitch holder
• tapestry needle, cotton thread

Notes

1 See *Techniques*, page 70, for garter-stitch grafting.
2 Scarf is made in 2 sections, then grafted together.
3 Instructions are for both scarves. If different, instructions for 1-ply scarf come first, with 2-ply scarf in parentheses.

SCARF

First Section

Cast on 67 stitches. Work chart rows 1–86 once. Place stitches on hold.

Second Section

Cast on 67 stitches. Work chart rows 1–93 once, then work 16-row repeat 19 (14) times. Work chart rows 24–31 once. Graft open stitches of 2 sections together.

JAMIESON & SMITH
*Shetland 1-ply Cobweb (wool; 15g; 215 yds)
or Shetland 2-ply Lace weight (wool; 30g; 250 yds) in White*

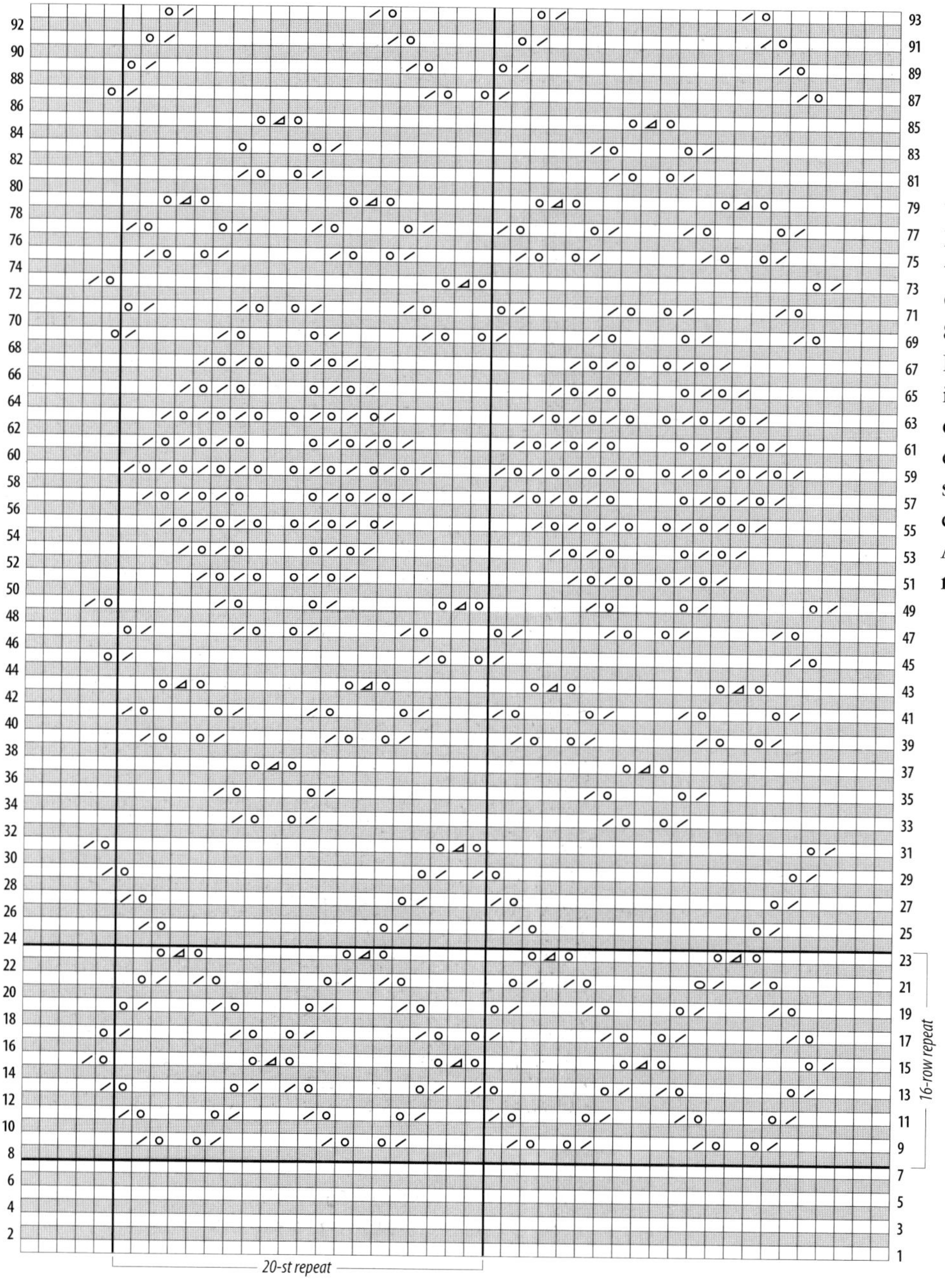

Finishing

Block scarf as follows: Fold scarf in half with cast-on edges together. Using cotton thread, overstitch the long sides of the scarf together, picking up the long threads between the garter stitch ridges. Cut a piece of cardboard 8½" × 17" (11" × 22"). Handwash scarf and roll in a clean towel to remove excess moisture. Pull scarf carefully over cardboard, stretching gently. Sew cast-on edges together. After scarf is dry, carefully remove stitching.

☐	K on RS
▨	K on WS
╱	K2tog
○	Yarn over
◿	K3tog

20-st repeat

16-row repeat

Simple triangles fall in line to form a rickrack pattern. The modular technique allows for sizing options in length, and gauge determines the scale and width. Make a scarf, sash, or armband. You are in control.

Designed by Knitter's Design Team

RickRack Scarf

Notes
1 See *Techniques,* page 70, for long-tail cast-on, SSK, and pick up and knit or purl. **2** If using more than 1 color, alternate colors of triangles as shown below.

SCARF
Left-slanting triangle (L)
Cast on 20 (12, 10) stitches.
Row 1 (WS) Knit.
Row 2 SSK, knit to end.
Repeat Rows 1 and 2 until 2 stitches remain. **Next row** (WS) K2. **Next row** SSK. Do not turn work.
Pick up and knit 19 (11, 9) stitches (in addition to the one on the right needle) along straight edge of triangle just finished. Repeat from * once more—one pair of left-slanting triangles and pick-up for right-slanting triangle complete.

Right-slanting triangle (R)
Row 1 (WS) Knit.
Row 2 Knit to last 2 stitches, k2tog.
Repeat Rows 1 and 2 until 2 stitches remain. **Next row** (WS) Knit. **Next row** K2tog. Turn work.
Pick up and purl 19 (11, 9) stitches (in addition to the one on the right needle) along straight edge of triangle just finished.
Row 1 (RS) Knit to last 2 stitches, k2tog.
Row 2 Knit.
Repeat Rows 1 and 2 until 2 stitches remain. **Next row** (RS) K2tog. Turn work—onc pair of right-slanting triangles complete.
Pick up and purl 19 (11, 9) stitches along straight edge of triangle just finished. Begin with Row 2 of left-slanting triangle and continue making pairs of left- and right-slanting triangles until 8 (16, 28) pairs have been made.
Fasten off last stitch. Block.

EASY +

WIDE • 8½" x 48"
MEDIUM • 4½" x 54"
NARROW • 2" x 41"
•approximate finished measurements

10cm/4"
32, 36, 56
16, 18, 32
• over garter stitch (knit every row)

1 2 **3-4** 5 6

Medium weight • 180 yds
Light weight • 160 yds
Super fine weight • 80 yds

• 5.5mm/US9
• 4mm/US7
• 2.75mm/US2
or size to obtain gauge

← direction of knitting
- - - - pick up and k or p
—— cast-on

58

Wide version PLYMOUTH
Bella Colour (cotton, acrylic; 50g; 104 yds) in 14

Medium version on page 60 DIAKETO
*Mim (polyester; 40g; 187 yds) in 723
and DIAKETO QL
(wool, silk, polyester; 40g; 126 yds) in 908*

Narrow version on page 60 TAHKI STACY
CHARLES
Dream (wool, nylon; 50g; 262 yds) in 10 Turquoise

Striped scarves are often plagued with the problem of where to hide the tails when changing from color to color. We solve that problem by working color changes at random within rows, and rather than hiding the ends, we knot them together and leave them as fringe wherever a color change happens.

Designed by Julie Gaddy

Family Wraps

EASY

Child's • 5½" x 40"
Woman's • 6¾" x 50"
Man's • 6¾" x 48"
• approximate finished measurements

10cm/4"

32, 25, 24
23, 19, 16

• over stockinette stitch
(knit on RS, purl on WS)
using respective needle size

1 2 **3** 4 5 6

• Light weight
MC • 246 yds
A, B • 123 yds each

1 2 3 **4** 5 6

• Medium weight
MC • 220 yds
A, B • 150 yds each
MC, A, B • 220 yds each

• 5.5mm/US9
• 4mm/US6
• 5.5mm/US9
or size to obtain gauge

62

Note

1 Use the illustrations and accompanying stitch charts as suggestions for stitch and color combinations and fringe placement. **2** When changing colors, drop first color to right side (RS) of work; join second color, leaving tail on RS.

CHILD'S SCARF

With MC, cast on 31 stitches. Knit 6 rows. Keeping first and last 3 stitches in garter stitch (knit every row) and center 25 stitches in random stripe and fringe pattern, work until piece measures 39" from beginning, ending with a WS row. Knit 6 rows. Bind off.

WOMAN'S SCARF

With MC, cast on 33 stitches.
Begin seed stitch: Row 1 (RS) * K1, p1; repeat from *, end k1.
Rows 2–4 Repeat Row 1.
Next row (RS) K1, [p1, k1] twice, k23, [k1, p1] twice, k1. Keeping first and last 5 stitches in seed stitch, and center 23 stitches in random stripe and fringe pattern, work until piece measures 49" from beginning, ending with a WS row. Work 5 rows in seed stitch over all stitches. Bind off.

MAN'S SCARF

With MC, cast on 29 stitches. Knit 6 rows. Keeping first and last 3 stitches in garter stitch (knit every row) and center 23 stitches in random stripe and fringe pattern, work until piece measures 47" from beginning, ending with a WS row. Knit 6 rows. Bind off.

Tips

- *Work the pattern over the center 25 (23, 23) stitches in random stockinette stitch and garter stripes and fringe, as desired.*
- *When changing colors in the middle of a row, pull the working yarn to the right side of the work and cut it, leaving a 4" tail. Join the new yarn, leaving a 4" tail on the right side. When the row is complete, tie an overhand knot to secure the ends. Leave the tails hanging on the right side, creating fringe.*
- *Stagger the fringe throughout the scarf by joining the new color after a different number of stitches each time.*
- *Trim the fringe to a uniform length after blocking. Be sure to trim fringe on child's scarf to no more than 2" to avoid the possibility of tangling in jacket zippers or playground equipment.*

□ K on RS, p on WS   ▬ P on RS, k on WS

Chart A

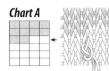

On a RS row, knit to color-change point, drop first color, join 2nd color and knit.

Chart B

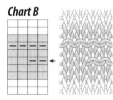

Combine knit and purl stitches in one row.

Chart C

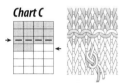

Work a RS row as for Chart A, then knit a WS row with another color.

Chart D

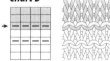

Knit a WS row with another color.

Chart E

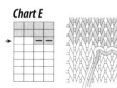

On a WS row, purl to color-change point, drop first color, join 2nd color and knit.

Chart F

On a WS row, knit to color-change point, drop first color, join 2nd color and purl.

ROWAN YARNS

Child's, center Wool Cotton (wool, cotton; 50g; 123 yds) in 911 Rich (MC), 946 Elf (A), and 950 Mango (B)

Woman's, right Kid Classic (lambswool, mohair, nylon; 50g; 151 yds) in 827 Juicy (MC), 829 Imp (A), and 817 Bear (B)

Man's, left Rowanspun Aran (wool; 100g; 219 yds) in 963 Shark (MC), 972 Hardy (A), and 970 Autumn (B)

This jaunty little scarf packs plenty of punch! It's a chic accessory that makes a great gift. Luxurious mohair/silk yarn and the added interest of short-row gussets give this quick-knit scarf wearing and knitting appeal.

Designed by Katharine Hunt

Shaped Ascot

it's easy ...go for it!

EASY +

Sizes S (L)

6" x 39" (6" x 42")
• approximate finished measurements

10cm/4"

33

16

• over garter stitch
(knit every row)

1 2 3 **4** 5 6

• Medium weight
• 264 yds each size

• 5.5mm/US9, or size to obtain gauge
74cm/29" long

Notes

1 See *Techniques*, page 70, for wrap and turn on short rows (W & T). **2** This ascot is designed to be given a twist when wearing (as shown in photo) in order for identical ends to be displayed.

ASCOT

Cast on 163 (171) stitches.
Begin short rows: Row 1 Knit.
Row 2 K16, W&T.
Row 3 Purl to end.
Row 4 K16, hide wrap (HW), knit to end.
Rows 5–7 Repeat Rows 2–4.
Rows 8 and 9 Knit.
Row 10 K24, W&T.
Row 11 Purl to end.
Row 12 K24, HW, knit to end.
Rows 13–15 Repeat Rows 10–12.
Row 16 Knit. Repeat Rows 1–16 four times more, then repeat Rows 1–9 once more. Bind off.

Finishing

Block piece.

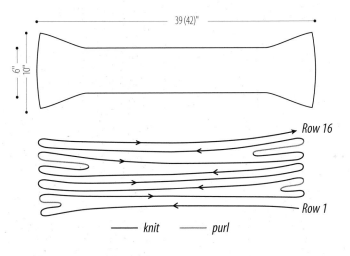

39 (42)"

6"
10"

Row 16

Row 1

—— *knit* —— *purl*

BROWN SHEEP Prairie Silk (wool,
mohair, silk; 50g; 88 yds)
in Franc Framboise

EASY

1 2 3 **4** 5 6

• Medium weight
SCARF 1 • 537 yds
SCARF 2 • 528 yds

SCARF 1 • 6.5mm/US10½
SCARF 2 • 8mm/US11

SCARVES 1 & 2
• 3.75mm/F-5

Make scarves using an assortment of interesting yarns. And if you choose a luxury fiber, you won't break the bank—these scarves all take a modest amount of yarn. The stitches are easy, and best of all, gauge isn't important. Using large needles, several can be worked in a few hours or days.

Spectacular Scarves

Note

See *Techniques*, page 70, for elongated stitch, fringe, loop cast-on, and making pompons.

SCARF 1

Cast on 50 stitches. Knit 7 rows.
Begin elongated stitch pattern: Row 1 (RS)
* K1, wrapping yarn twice around needle (instead of once); repeat from *.
Row 2 * K1, dropping wraps; repeat from *.
Rows 3 and 4 Knit. Repeat Rows 1–4 until scarf measures 59", ending with Row 4. Knit 4 rows. Bind off.
Work double-knotted fringe
Work 21 sections of 8-strand, 12" fringe along cast-on and bound-off edges, then work double-knotted fringe.

SCARF 2

Cast on 49 stitches.
Begin pattern stitch: Row 1 (RS) * P1, k3; repeat from *, end p1.
Row 2 K2, * p1, k3; repeat from * to last 3 stitches, p1, k2. Repeat Rows 1–2 until scarf measures 52". Bind off.

Scarf 1 designed by Julie Gaddy
LION BRAND *Imagine (acrylic, mohair; 56g; 179 yds) in Norwegian Wood*

Scarf 2 designed by Kathy Cheifetz
BROWN SHEEP *Prairie Silk (wool, mohair, silk; 50g; 88 yds) in Real Royal*

it's easy ...go for it!

24

Work fringe

Work 13 sections of 6-strand, 8" fringe along cast-on and bound-off edges, working 1 section on each raised knit rib at each edge.

SCARF 3

Strip A With A, cast on 30 stitches, leaving an 18" tail. Work 6" in stockinette stitch (knit on RS, purl on WS), end with a WS row.
* ***Next row*** (RS) K14, bind off 2 stitches, knit to end.
Next row P14, loop cast on 2 stitches, purl to end. Work 12" even. Repeat from * 4 times more. Do not bind off. Run yarn through stitches and pull together tightly. Gather stitches at cast-on edge by running 18" tail through stitches and pulling together tightly.
Strip B With B, work as for Strip A.
Lay strips side by side with eyelets alternating (see diagram). * Pass Strip B down through first eyelet in Strip A and out to left. Pass Strip A down through first eyelet in Strip B and out to left. Repeat from * to end of scarf. Make 4 pompons (2 of each color) and attach to ends of scarf, alternating colors.

Scarf 3 *designed by Susan Guagliumi BEROCCO Furz (nylon, wool, acrylic; 50g; 90 yds) in Granite (A) and Ripe Eggplant (B)*

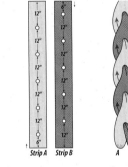

Scarf 4 COLINETTE *Point Five (wool; 100g; 54 yds) in Summer Berries*

Scarf 5 MUENCH GGH *Gala (Tactel nylon; 50g; 93 yds) in Eggplant*

Scarf 6 SKACEL *Luxor (wool, acrylic, nylon; 50g; 58 yds) in Blue Variegated*

SCARF 4

Cast on 16 stitches. * Knit 3 rows. Purl 1 row. Repeat from * until scarf measures 60". Bind off.

Work fringe

Work 9 sections of 4-strand, 9" fringe along cast-on and bound-off edges.

SCARF 5

Cast on 24 stitches.
Row 1 (RS) Knit.
Row 2 K1, purl to last stitch, k1. Repeat Rows 1 and 2 until scarf measures 58". Bind off.

SCARF 6

Cast on 33 stitches.
Row 1 (RS) * K3, p3; repeat from *, end k3.
Row 2 * P3, k3; repeat from *, end p3.
Repeat Rows 1 and 2 until scarf measures 46". Bind off.

SCARF 7

Cast on 20 stitches. Knit every row until scarf measures 72". Bind off.

Scarf 7 AURORA GARNSTUDIO *Leopard (polyacrylic; 100g; 121 yds) in Brown Tweed*

SCARVES 6 & 7 • EASY

1 2 3 4 **5-6**

• Bulky–Super Bulky weight
SCARF 6 • 232 yds
SCARF 7 • 242 yds

SCARF 6 • 8mm/US11
SCARF 7 •10mm/US15

69

TECHNIQUES INDEX

KNIT CAST-ON

1 Start with a slipknot on left needle (first cast-on stitch). Insert right needle into slipknot from front. Wrap yarn over right needle as if to knit.

2 Bring yarn through slipknot, forming a loop on right needle.
3 Insert left needle **under** loop and slip loop off right needle. One additional stitch cast on.

4 Insert right needle into the last stitch on left needle as if to knit. Knit a stitch and transfer it to the left needle as in Step 3. Repeat Step 4 for each additional stitch.

CABLE CAST-ON

1–2 Work as for Steps 1 and 2 of Knit Cast-on.
3 Insert left needle in loop and slip loop off right needle. One additional stitch cast on.

4 Insert right needle **between** the last 2 stitches. From this position, knit a stitch and slip it to the left needle as in Step 3. Repeat Step 4 for each additional stitch.

LOOP CAST-ON (ALSO CALLED E-WRAP CAST-ON)

Often used to cast on a few stitches, as for a buttonhole
1 Hold needle and tail in left hand.
2 Bring right index finger under yarn, pointing toward you.

3 Turn index finger to point away from you.
4 Insert tip of needle under yarn on index finger (see above); remove finger and draw yarn snug, forming a stitch. Repeat Steps 2–4 until all stitches are on needle.

INVISIBLE CAST-ON

A temporary cast-on
1 Knot working yarn to contrasting waste yarn. Hold needle and knot in right hand. Tension both strands in left hand; separate strands so waste yarn is over index finger, working yarn over thumb. Bring needle between strands and under thumb yarn so working yarn forms a yarn-over in front of waste yarn.

2 Holding both yarns taut, pivot hand toward you, bringing working yarn under and behind waste yarn. Bring needle behind and under working yarn so working yarn forms a yarn-over behind waste yarn.

3 Pivot hand away from you, bringing working yarn under and in front of waste yarn. Bring needle between strands and under working yarn, forming a yarn-over in front of waste yarn. Each yarn-over forms a stitch.
Repeat Steps 2–3 for required number of stitches. For an even number, twist working yarn around waste strand before knitting the first row.

CHAIN CAST-ON

A temporary cast-on
1 With crochet hook and waste yarn, loosely chain the number of stitches needed, plus a few extra chains. Cut yarn.
2 With needle and main yarn, pick up and knit 1 stitch into the back 'purl bump' of the first

chain. Continue, knitting 1 stitch into each chain until you have the required number of stitches. Do not work into remaining chains.

ELONGATED STITCH

1 Knit 1, EXCEPT wrap yarn 2 or more times around needle, instead of once, before drawing new stitch through old stitch.

2 On next row, knit the stitch, dropping extra wrap(s) as stitch is pulled off left needle.

CROCHET CHAIN STITCH (ch st, ch)

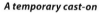

1 Make a slipknot to begin.
2 Catch yarn and draw through loop on hook.

First chain made. Repeat Step 2.

ABBREVIATIONS

CC contrasting color
cn cable needle
cm centimeter(s)
dec decreas(e)(ed)(es)(ing)
dpn double-pointed needle(s)
g gram(s)
" inch(es)
inc increas(e)(ed)(es)(ing)
k knit(ting)(s)(ted)
LH left-hand
M1 Make one stitch (increase)
m meter(s)
mm millimeter(s)
MC main color
oz ounce(s)
p purl(ed)(ing)(s) or page
pm place marker
psso pass slipped stitch(es) over
RH right-hand
RS right side(s)
sc single crochet
sl slip(ped)(ping)
SKP slip, knit, psso
SSK slip, slip, knit these 2 sts tog
SSP slip, slip, purl these 2 sts tog
st(s) stitch(es)
St st stockinette stitch
tbl through back of loop(s)
WS wrong side(s)
wyib with yarn in back
wyif with yarn in front
yd(s) yard(s)
yo(2) yarn over (twice)

PICK UP AND KNIT

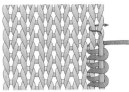

Insert needle in space **between** first and second stitches, catch yarn and knit a stitch.

KNIT, PURL THROUGH BACK LOOP (k1 tbl, p1 tbl)

1 With right needle behind left needle and right leg of stitch, insert needle into stitch…

2 …and **knit**.

Or, with right needle behind left needle, insert right needle into stitch from left to right and **purl**.

KNIT INTO FRONT AND BACK (kf&b)

1 Knit into the front of next stitch on left needle, but do not pull the stitch off the needle.
2 Take right needle to back, then knit through the back of the same stitch.

3 Pull stitch off left needle. Completed increase: 2 stitches from 1 stitch. This increase results in a purl bump after the knit stitch.

YARN-OVER (yo)

Between knit stitches
Bring yarn under needle to the front, take it over the needle to the back and knit the next stitch.

Completed yo increase.

SINGLE CROCHET (sc)

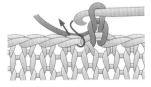

1 Insert hook into a stitch, catch yarn, and pull up a loop. Catch yarn and pull through the loop on the hook.
2 Insert hook into next stitch to the left.

3 Catch yarn and pull through the stitch; 2 loops on hook.

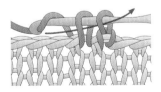

4 Catch yarn and pull through both loops on hook; 1 single crochet completed. Repeat Steps 2–4.

DECREASES

SLIP PURLWISE (sl 1 p-wise)

1 Insert right needle into next stitch on left needle from back to front (as if to purl).

2 Slide stitch from left to right needle. Stitch orientation does not change (right leg of stitch loop is at front of needle).

K2tog

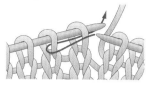

1 Insert right needle into first 2 stitches on left needle, beginning with second stitch from end of left needle.

2 Knit these 2 stitches together as if they were 1.
The result is a right-slanting decrease.

SLIP KNITWISE (sl 1 k-wise)

1 Insert right needle into next stitch on left needle from front to back (as if to knit).

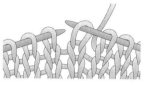

2 Slide stitch from left to right needle. Stitch orientation changes (right leg of stitch loop is at back of needle).

The stitch slipped knitwise can be a knit or a purl.

SK2P, sl 1-k2tog-psso

1 Slip 1 stitch knitwise.
2 Knit next 2 stitches together.
3 Pass the slipped stitch over the k2tog: 3 stitches become 1; the right stitch is on top.
The result is a left-slanting double decrease.

SSK

1 Slip 2 stitches **separately** to right needle as if to knit.

2 Slip left needle into these 2 stitches from left to right and knit them together: 2 stitches become 1.

The result is a left-slanting decrease.

SHORT ROWS

Each short row adds 2 rows of knitting across a section of the work. Since the work is turned before completing a row, stitches must be wrapped at the turn to prevent holes. Wrap and turn as follows:

 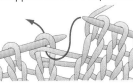  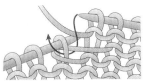

Knit side

1 With yarn in back, slip next stitch as if to purl. Bring yarn to front of work and slip stitch back to left needle (as shown). Turn work.
2 With yarn in front, slip next stitch as if to purl. Work to end.

3 When you come to the wrap on a following knit row, hide the wrap by knitting it together with the stitch it wraps.

Purl side

1 With yarn in front, slip next stitch as if to purl. Bring yarn to back of work and slip stitch back to left needle (as shown). Turn work.
2 With yarn in back, slip next stitch as if to purl. Work to end.

3 When you come to the wrap on a following purl row, hide the wrap by purling it together with the stitch it wraps.

ADDING BEADS

Using a loop of thread or fine wire, string required number of beads (or sequins) on yarn.

POMPONS

 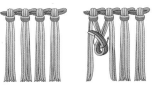

1 Cut 2 pieces of cardboard half the desired width of the pompon.
2 Place a length of yarn between cardboard pieces.
3 Hold the pieces together and wrap yarn around them.

4 Tie the length of yarn tightly at one edge.
5 Cut the wrapped yarn on opposite side.

6 Remove cardboard, fluff, and trim pompon.
7 Use ties to attach.

ATTACHING FRINGE

Cut lengths of yarn to twice desired length of fringe plus 1". Divide into groups of 2 or more strands.
1 Insert crochet hook from wrong side of work through a stitch at edge. Draw center of strands through, forming a loop.

2 Draw ends through loop. One fringe section complete.

DOUBLE-KNOTTED FRINGE

1 Attach fringe along edge.
2 Using half the strands from first section and half from the next section, tie an overhand knot approximately 1" below edge of scarf. Repeat Step 2 across.
3 Work another row of knots 1" below 2nd row of knots.

BIND OFF KNITWISE

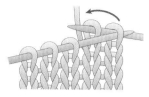

1 Knit 2 stitches as usual.
2 With left needle, pass first stitch on right needle over second stitch…

… and off needle: 1 stitch bound off (see above).
3 Knit 1 more stitch.
4 Pass first stitch over second. Repeat Steps 3–4.

BIND OFF PURLWISE

Work Steps 1–4 of Bind off knitwise EXCEPT, purl the stitches instead of knitting them.

BIND OFF IN PATTERN

As you work the bind-off row for fabrics other than stockinette and garter stitch, knit or purl the stitches as the pattern requires.

GRAFT IN GARTER

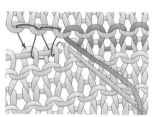

1 Arrange stitches on 2 needles so stitches on lower, or front, needle come out of purl bumps and stitches on the upper, or back, needle come out of smooth knits.
2 Thread a blunt needle with matching yarn (approximately 1" per stitch).
3 Working from right to left, begin with Steps 3a and 3b:
3a *Front needle:* bring yarn through first stitch *as if to purl,* leave stitch **on needle.**
3b *Back needle:* repeat Step 3a.
4a *Front needle:* bring yarn through first stitch *as if to knit, slip off* needle; through next stitch *as if to purl, leave on* needle.
4b *Back needle:* repeat Step 4a. Repeat Steps 4a and 4b until 1 stitch remains on each needle.
5a *Front needle:* bring yarn through stitch *as if to knit,* slip *off needle.*
5b *Back needle:* repeat Step 5a.
6 Adjust tension to match rest of knitting.

GRAFT IN STOCKINETTE

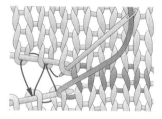

1 Arrange stitches on 2 needles as shown.
2 Thread a blunt needle with matching yarn (approximately 1" per stitch).
3 Working from right to left, with right sides facing you, begin with Steps 3a and 3b:
3a *Front needle:* bring yarn through first stitch *as if to purl,* leave stitch **on needle.**
3b *Back needle:* bring yarn through first stitch *as if to knit,* leave stitch **on needle.**
4a *Front needle:* bring yarn through first stitch *as if to knit, slip off* needle; through next stitch *as if to purl,* leave stitch **on needle.**
4b *Back needle:* bring yarn through first stitch *as if to purl, slip off* needle; through next stitch *as if to knit,* leave stitch **on needle.**
Repeat Steps 4a and 4b until 1 stitch remains on each needle.
5a *Front needle:* bring yarn through stitch *as if to knit,* slip *off needle.*
5b *Back needle:* bring yarn through stitch *as if to purl,* slip *off needle.*
6 Adjust tension to match rest of knitting.

Specifications:

Left column (Specifications key)

INTERMEDIATE

One size
9" x 20"
measurements are approximate
10cm/4"

27
21
• over stockinette stitch
(k on RS, p on WS)

1 2 3 **4** 5 6

• Medium weight
MC, A, B, C, D, E, F • 88 yds each

• Four 4.5mm/US7 double-pointed needles
(dpn), or size to obtain gauge

• 4.5mm/US7 circular 40cm (16") long

&

• Stitch marker, yarn needle

Middle column (Labels)

Skill level

Size
  and measurements

Gauge
  *The number of stitches and
  rows you need in 10 cm or
  4", worked as specified.*

Yarn weight
  and amount in yards

Type of needles
  *Straight, unless circular
  or double-pointed
  are recommended.*

Any extras

Conversion chart

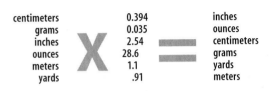

centimeters	0.394	inches
grams	0.035	ounces
inches	2.54	centimeters
ounces	28.6	grams
meters	1.1	yards
yards	.91	meters

Needles/Hooks

US	MM	HOOK
0	2	A
1	2.25	B
2	2.75	C
3	3.25	D
4	3.5	E
5	3.75	F
6	4	G
7	4.5	7
8	5	H
9	5.5	I
10	6	J
10½	6.5	K
11	8	L
13	9	M
15	10	N
17	12.75	

Equivalent weights

¾ oz		20 g
1 oz		28 g
1½ oz		40 g
1¾ oz		50 g
2 oz		60 g
3½ oz		100 g

At a Glance

Yarn substitutions

Throughout this book, the photo caption describes the yarns and colors in the photograph. If a yarn is not available, its yardage and content information will help in making a substitution. Locate the Yarn Weight and Stockinette Stitch Gauge Range over 10cm to 4" on the chart. Compare that range with the information on the yarn label to find an appropriate yarn. These are guidelines only for commonly used gauges and needle sizes in specific yarn categories.

Measuring Gauge

10cm/4"

24 ▦ *GET GAUGE!*

18

• *over pattern stitch*
• *after blocking*

• Cast on a minimum of 5" worth of stitches.
• Work 2 rows of *knit*, continue to work in pattern specified for 5", then work 2 rows of knit.
Measure the swatch
• Steam or wash the swatch as you will the scarf; after drying, measure the swatch, then count the stitches and the rows in 4".
• If your stitches number less than the pattern's, your stitches are too large and you should try a swatch with a smaller-sized needle.
• If your stitches number more than the pattern's, your stitches are too small and you should try a swatch with a larger-sized needle.
• If your rows number 1 or 2 less than the pattern's, try a swatch with the next smaller-sized needle. This may give you the correct row gauge without affecting the stitch gauge.
• If your rows number 1 or 2 more than the pattern's, try a swatch with the next larger-sized needle. This may give you the correct row gauge without affecting the stitch gauge.

TIP
Even if your gauge swatch is correct, don't stop measuring. Periodically measure the piece you are working on. Your gauge can change as you are working.

Yarn weight categories

Yarn Weight

1	**2**	**3**	**4**	**5**	**6**
Super Fine	**Fine**	**Light**	**Medium**	**Bulky**	**Super Bulky**

Also called

Sock Fingering Baby	Sport Baby	DK Light-Worsted	Worsted Afghan Aran	Chunky Craft Rug	Bulky Roving

Stockinette Stitch Gauge Range 10cm/4 inches

27 sts to 32 sts	23 sts to 26 sts	21 sts to 24 sts	16 sts to 20 sts	12 sts to 15 sts	6 sts to 11 sts

Recommended needle (metric)

2.25 mm to 3.25 mm	3.25 mm to 3.75 mm	3.75 mm to 4.5 mm	4.5 mm to 5.5 mm	5.5 mm to 8 mm	8 mm and larger

Recommended needle (US)

1 to 3	3 to 5	5 to 7	7 to 9	9 to 11	11 and larger

A special thank you to our Knitter's Kids for modeling. Hannah, Nevada, Zac, Spencer, Jack, and Ryan, we loved spending the weekend with you and your Moms— Julie, Lisa and Natalie.

Bags
- a Knitter's dozen

ponchos & wraps
- a Knitter's dozen

Scarves
- a Knitter's dozen

- the Knitter's dozen series

The Best of Knitter's
ARANS & CELTICS
SHAWLS & SCARVES

A Knitter's Dozen
ANGELS
BAGS
HATS
PONCHOS & WRAPS
SCARVES

The Knitting Experience
BOOK 1: THE KNIT STITCH
BOOK 2: THE PURL STITCH

A GATHERING OF LACE

ETHNIC
SOCKS & STOCKINGS

JEAN FROST
JACKETS

KIDS KIDS KIDS

KNITTER'S
SCHOOL HANDBOOK

MAGGIE'S IRELAND

MAGNIFICENT MITTENS

MODULE MAGIC

THE BEST OF LOPI

TWO SWEATERS
FOR MY FATHER

SCULPTURED KNITS

SOCKS SOCKS SOCKS

STYLES

EXPLORE

Knitter's thumb-through

Knitter's Thumb-through

Did you know you could thumb through the pages of XRX Books? **Knitter's Thumb-through** is the online answer to "try before you buy!"

Knitter's Paint Box

Have you dabbled in digital paint? Work out the available patterns any way you like, then print the results.

INTERACT

ENJOY

www.knittinguniverse.com

The online home of
XRX Books, Knitter's Magazine,
and Stitches Events

Contributors

Kathy Cheifetz

Lily M Chin

Evelyn Clark

Julie Gaddy

Susan Guagliumi

Robyn Hamilton

Katharine Hunt

Dana Hurt

Patricia Kalthoff

Mary Kay

Rick Mondragon

Jean Schafer-Albers

Terri Shea

Susan Wills